EMMANUEL JOSEPH

From Coins to Conquests Building Global Empires on Blockchain's Edge

Copyright © 2025 by Emmanuel Joseph

All rights reserved. No part of this publication may be reproduced, stored or transmitted in any form or by any means, electronic, mechanical, photocopying, recording, scanning, or otherwise without written permission from the publisher. It is illegal to copy this book, post it to a website, or distribute it by any other means without permission.

First edition

This book was professionally typeset on Reedsy.
Find out more at reedsy.com

Contents

1. Chapter 1 — 1
2. Chapter 1: The Genesis of a Revolution — 3
3. Chapter 2: The Rise of Decentralized Economies — 4
4. Chapter 3: The Battle for Sovereignty — 6
5. Chapter 4: The Age of Tokenization — 7
6. Chapter 5: The Decentralized Society — 9
7. Chapter 6: The Environmental Crossroads — 10
8. Chapter 7: Quantum Computing and the Blockchain Frontier — 11
9. Chapter 8: The Role of Artificial Intelligence — 12
10. Chapter 9: The Future of Work — 14
11. Chapter 10: The Ethics of Decentralization — 15
12. Chapter 11: Blockchain and Space Exploration — 16
13. Chapter 12: The Blockchain-Powered Utopia — 17

Chapter 1

Introduction: The Dawn of a New Era

Imagine a world where power is not held by a few but distributed among many. A world where trust is not granted to institutions but encoded in technology. A world where borders fade, and opportunities are limitless. This is the promise of blockchain—a revolutionary technology that has quietly reshaped the foundations of our global society.

From Coins to Conquests: Building Global Empires on Blockchain's Edge is not just a book about technology; it is a story of human ambition, innovation, and the relentless pursuit of a better future. It begins with a simple idea: a decentralized ledger that records transactions without the need for intermediaries. But this idea has grown into something far greater—a tool for building empires, not of land or gold, but of trust, transparency, and collaboration.

Blockchain's journey is a testament to the power of human ingenuity. From its humble beginnings as the backbone of Bitcoin, it has evolved into a force that touches every aspect of our lives. It has redefined money, challenged traditional power structures, and created new opportunities for people around the world. It has sparked debates about sovereignty, ethics, and the future of work. And it has inspired a global movement of pioneers, dreamers, and builders who believe in its potential to create a more equitable and inclusive world.

But this journey has not been without its challenges. Blockchain has faced skepticism, resistance, and even hostility. It has been criticized for its environmental impact, its association with illicit activities, and its potential to disrupt established systems. Yet, despite these obstacles, it has persevered, driven by the belief that technology can be a force for good.

This book is an exploration of that journey. It is a celebration of the triumphs and a reflection on the struggles. It is a call to action for those who dare to imagine a better world and a guide for those who seek to build it. Whether you are a seasoned technologist, a curious observer, or a skeptic, this book invites you to join the conversation and be part of the revolution.

The dawn of the blockchain era is here. The question is not whether it will change the world—it already has. The question is how we will shape its future. Let us begin.

2

Chapter 1: The Genesis of a Revolution

The world was on the brink of a transformation. In 2009, an anonymous figure known as Satoshi Nakamoto introduced Bitcoin, a decentralized digital currency built on blockchain technology. This innovation was more than just a new form of money; it was a rebellion against centralized financial systems. For centuries, empires had been built on gold, oil, and fiat currencies, but blockchain promised a new foundation—transparency, security, and decentralization.

Early adopters were a mix of idealists, tech enthusiasts, and skeptics. They saw blockchain as a tool to disrupt traditional power structures. The first Bitcoin transactions were humble—pizzas bought for 10,000 BTC—but they hinted at a future where value could be transferred without intermediaries. The blockchain was not just a ledger; it was a manifesto for a new world order.

As the technology gained traction, its potential became clear. Blockchain was not limited to currency. It could record contracts, verify identities, and even track supply chains. The seeds of a global revolution had been planted, and the world would never be the same.

Yet, challenges loomed. Governments questioned its legality, banks dismissed it as a fad, and criminals exploited its anonymity. But the pioneers pressed on, driven by a vision of a fairer, more inclusive financial system. The journey from coins to conquests had begun.

3

Chapter 2: The Rise of Decentralized Economies

By the mid-2010s, blockchain had evolved beyond Bitcoin. Ethereum introduced smart contracts, enabling programmable transactions and decentralized applications (dApps). This innovation opened the door to a new era of economic activity. Entrepreneurs began building decentralized finance (DeFi) platforms, allowing users to lend, borrow, and trade without banks.

These platforms were not without risks. Hacks and scams were common, and regulatory uncertainty created volatility. But for every setback, there was a breakthrough. Stablecoins emerged, pegging cryptocurrencies to fiat currencies and reducing volatility. Tokenization allowed real-world assets like real estate and art to be traded on the blockchain.

The rise of decentralized economies challenged traditional institutions. Banks, once the gatekeepers of finance, found themselves competing with open-source protocols. Governments, too, had to adapt, exploring central bank digital currencies (CBDCs) to maintain control over monetary policy.

For individuals, blockchain offered unprecedented opportunities. Farmers in developing countries could access microloans, artists could monetize their work through NFTs, and workers could receive payments in cryptocurrencies without relying on unstable local currencies. The global economy was

CHAPTER 2: THE RISE OF DECENTRALIZED ECONOMIES

becoming more inclusive, one block at a time.

Yet, the road ahead was uncertain. Scalability issues, energy consumption, and regulatory hurdles threatened to slow progress. But the pioneers remained undeterred, driven by the belief that blockchain could reshape the world.

4

Chapter 3: The Battle for Sovereignty

As blockchain gained momentum, it became a battleground for sovereignty. Nations vied for dominance in this new digital frontier. Some, like El Salvador, embraced Bitcoin as legal tender, betting on its potential to boost economic growth. Others, like China, cracked down on cryptocurrencies while developing their own CBDCs.

The battle was not just between nations but also between ideologies. Libertarians saw blockchain as a tool to escape government control, while technocrats viewed it as a way to modernize governance. The tension between decentralization and regulation became a defining feature of the blockchain era.

Corporations, too, entered the fray. Tech giants like Facebook (now Meta) announced their own digital currencies, sparking debates about privacy and monopolization. Meanwhile, startups aimed to create decentralized alternatives to traditional services, from social media to cloud storage.

The stakes were high. Whoever controlled the blockchain could shape the future of finance, governance, and even identity. The battle for sovereignty was not just about power; it was about the kind of world humanity wanted to build.

Amid the chaos, one thing was clear: blockchain was no longer a niche technology. It was a global force, reshaping the balance of power in ways no one could have predicted.

5

Chapter 4: The Age of Tokenization

Tokenization emerged as one of blockchain's most transformative applications. By converting physical and digital assets into tokens, blockchain made it possible to trade anything from real estate to intellectual property on a global scale. This innovation democratized access to wealth, enabling anyone with an internet connection to participate in the global economy.

Artists and creators were among the first to embrace tokenization. NFTs (non-fungible tokens) allowed them to monetize their work directly, bypassing traditional gatekeepers like galleries and record labels. For collectors, NFTs offered a new way to own and trade unique digital assets.

The impact extended beyond art. Tokenization revolutionized industries like real estate, where fractional ownership made high-value properties accessible to smaller investors. It also transformed supply chains, enabling companies to track goods from production to delivery with unprecedented transparency.

But tokenization was not without controversy. Critics argued that it fueled speculation and inequality, with some NFTs selling for millions while others languished in obscurity. Environmental concerns also arose, as the energy-intensive nature of blockchain clashed with the growing demand for sustainability.

Despite these challenges, tokenization continued to gain traction. It was a testament to blockchain's potential to redefine ownership and value in the digital age.

6

Chapter 5: The Decentralized Society

By the late 2020s, blockchain had permeated every aspect of society. Decentralized autonomous organizations (DAOs) emerged as a new form of governance, allowing communities to make decisions without centralized authority. These organizations ranged from small collectives to massive networks managing billions of dollars in assets.

The concept of identity also evolved. Blockchain-based digital IDs gave individuals control over their personal data, reducing the risk of identity theft and enabling seamless cross-border transactions. Refugees, in particular, benefited from this innovation, as they could carry their identities and assets on a smartphone.

Education and healthcare were transformed as well. Blockchain verified academic credentials, making it easier for students to prove their qualifications. In healthcare, it secured patient records and streamlined data sharing between providers.

Yet, the decentralized society was not without its flaws. The lack of central authority sometimes led to chaos, and the digital divide excluded those without access to technology. But for many, the benefits outweighed the risks.

Blockchain had become more than a technology; it was a movement, a philosophy, and a way of life. The world was no longer divided by borders but connected by blocks, forging a new kind of global empire.

7

Chapter 6: The Environmental Crossroads

As blockchain technology expanded, its environmental impact came under scrutiny. The energy consumption of proof-of-work (PoW) systems, like Bitcoin, became a lightning rod for criticism. Critics argued that the carbon footprint of mining operations was unsustainable, especially in the face of climate change.

The blockchain community responded with innovation. Proof-of-stake (PoS) and other consensus mechanisms emerged, drastically reducing energy consumption. Ethereum's transition to PoS was a landmark moment, cutting its energy use by over 99%. Renewable energy solutions also gained traction, with mining operations powered by solar, wind, and hydroelectric energy.

Governments and corporations joined the effort, setting sustainability standards for blockchain projects. Carbon offset programs and green certifications became common, as the industry sought to balance growth with environmental responsibility.

Yet, the debate continued. Some argued that blockchain's energy use was justified by its potential to create a more equitable world. Others called for stricter regulations to ensure sustainability. The environmental crossroads forced the blockchain community to confront its impact on the planet and innovate for a greener future.

8

Chapter 7: Quantum Computing and the Blockchain Frontier

The rise of quantum computing posed both a threat and an opportunity for blockchain. Quantum computers, with their immense processing power, could potentially break the cryptographic algorithms that secure blockchain networks. This vulnerability sparked fears of a "quantum apocalypse" that could undermine the entire system.

But blockchain developers were already preparing for the quantum era. Post-quantum cryptography emerged as a solution, creating algorithms resistant to quantum attacks. Researchers and startups raced to develop quantum-resistant blockchains, ensuring the technology's longevity.

At the same time, quantum computing offered new possibilities for blockchain. It could enhance scalability, optimize consensus mechanisms, and enable more complex smart contracts. The synergy between quantum computing and blockchain promised to unlock unprecedented levels of innovation.

The race to harness quantum computing became a defining challenge of the 2030s. Nations and corporations invested heavily in research, recognizing that the future of blockchain—and perhaps the global economy—depended on staying ahead of the quantum curve.

9

Chapter 8: The Role of Artificial Intelligence

Artificial intelligence (AI) and blockchain became inseparable partners in the quest for global transformation. AI algorithms optimized blockchain networks, improving efficiency and security. They also enabled predictive analytics, helping users make informed decisions in decentralized markets.

Blockchain, in turn, provided a secure and transparent framework for AI. It ensured the integrity of data used to train AI models, addressing concerns about bias and manipulation. Smart contracts automated AI-driven processes, from supply chain management to healthcare diagnostics.

Together, AI and blockchain reshaped industries. Autonomous organizations used AI to make decisions, while blockchain ensured accountability. AI-powered marketplaces matched buyers and sellers with unparalleled precision, and blockchain verified transactions in real time.

Yet, the partnership was not without challenges. Ethical concerns arose about the concentration of power in AI-blockchain systems. Who controlled the algorithms? Who owned the data? These questions sparked debates about governance and equity in the digital age.

The fusion of AI and blockchain marked a new era of innovation, but it also demanded a new social contract—one that balanced progress with responsibility.

10

Chapter 9: The Future of Work

Blockchain redefined the nature of work in the 21st century. Decentralized platforms enabled gig workers to connect directly with clients, bypassing traditional intermediaries. Smart contracts ensured fair payment, while blockchain-based reputations systems built trust in the digital economy.

The rise of DAOs created new opportunities for collaboration. Workers from around the world could contribute to projects and share in the rewards, regardless of their location. This global workforce was more flexible and inclusive than ever before.

But the future of work was not without challenges. Automation and AI threatened to displace jobs, while the gig economy raised concerns about job security and benefits. Blockchain offered solutions, such as universal basic income (UBI) funded by decentralized networks, but implementing these ideas required careful planning.

Education also evolved to meet the demands of the blockchain era. Online platforms offered blockchain-specific training, empowering workers to thrive in the digital economy. Lifelong learning became the norm, as individuals adapted to the rapid pace of technological change.

The future of work was uncertain, but one thing was clear: blockchain had the potential to create a more equitable and dynamic labor market.

11

Chapter 10: The Ethics of Decentralization

Decentralization was the cornerstone of blockchain's promise, but it also raised profound ethical questions. Without central authority, who was accountable for mistakes or abuses? How could decentralized systems ensure fairness and justice?

These questions became increasingly urgent as blockchain expanded into governance, healthcare, and other critical areas. DAOs faced challenges in decision-making, with some communities struggling to reach consensus. Blockchain-based voting systems promised transparency but also raised concerns about privacy and coercion.

The ethical debate extended to wealth distribution. While blockchain democratized access to financial systems, it also created new forms of inequality. Early adopters amassed vast fortunes, while others struggled to navigate the complex technology.

Philosophers, technologists, and policymakers grappled with these issues, seeking to balance the benefits of decentralization with the need for accountability. The ethics of decentralization became a central theme in the blockchain narrative, shaping its evolution and impact.

12

Chapter 11: Blockchain and Space Exploration

Blockchain's reach extended beyond Earth as humanity ventured into space. Space agencies and private companies used blockchain to manage resources, track equipment, and coordinate missions. Decentralized networks ensured secure communication between Earth and space, enabling real-time collaboration.

Blockchain also played a key role in the space economy. Tokenized assets, such as lunar land and asteroid minerals, created new investment opportunities. Space tourism companies used blockchain to manage bookings and payments, while decentralized platforms facilitated research and innovation.

The integration of blockchain and space exploration symbolized humanity's boundless ambition. It was a testament to the technology's versatility and its potential to shape the future—not just on Earth, but across the cosmos.

13

Chapter 12: The Blockchain-Powered Utopia

By the mid-21st century, blockchain had transformed the world. It had redefined money, governance, and identity, creating a more transparent, inclusive, and efficient global society. Decentralized systems empowered individuals, while blockchain's immutable ledger ensured trust and accountability.

Yet, the blockchain-powered utopia was not without its flaws. Challenges remained, from environmental sustainability to ethical governance. The technology was a tool, not a panacea, and its impact depended on how humanity chose to use it.

The journey from coins to conquests was far from over. As blockchain continued to evolve, it promised new possibilities and new challenges. The story of blockchain was the story of humanity itself—a tale of innovation, struggle, and the relentless pursuit of a better world.

Book Description: *From Coins to Conquests: Building Global Empires on Blockchain's Edge*

Imagine a technology so powerful that it can redefine money, reshape governance, and reimagine the very fabric of society. Imagine a tool that empowers individuals, challenges empires, and bridges divides. This is the story of blockchain—a story that begins with a single idea and grows into a global movement.

From Coins to Conquests: Building Global Empires on Blockchain's Edge is a deeply human exploration of one of the most transformative technologies of our time. It is not just a tale of code and algorithms but of people—visionaries, rebels, and builders—who dared to dream of a better world. It is a story of struggle and triumph, of innovation and adaptation, and of the endless possibilities that emerge when humanity harnesses the power of technology.

This book takes you on a journey through the rise of blockchain, from its origins as the foundation of Bitcoin to its evolution into a force that touches every corner of our lives. You'll discover how blockchain is reshaping finance, creating decentralized economies, and challenging traditional power structures. You'll explore its impact on identity, governance, and even space exploration. And you'll confront the ethical dilemmas, environmental challenges, and societal shifts that come with this new era.

But *From Coins to Conquests* is more than a chronicle of technological progress. It is a call to action. It invites you to imagine a world where trust is built into systems, where opportunities are accessible to all, and where the boundaries of what is possible are constantly expanding. It challenges you to think critically about the future we are building and the role you can play in shaping it.

Written in an engaging and accessible style, this book is for anyone curious about the blockchain revolution—whether you're a seasoned expert, a curious newcomer, or someone in between. It is a guide, a manifesto, and a source of inspiration for those who believe in the power of technology to create a better world.

The blockchain era is here. The question is no longer *if* it will change the world, but *how*. Will we use it to build empires of exclusion and control, or will we harness its potential to create a more equitable and inclusive future? The choice is ours.

www.ingramcontent.com/pod-product-compliance
Lightning Source LLC
LaVergne TN
LVHW020509080526
838202LV00057B/6258